Native Americans

Powhatan Indians

Suzanne Morgan Williams

Heinemann Library
Chicago, Illinois

Customer Service 888-454-2279

Visit our website at www.heinemannlibrary.com

Photo research by Amor Montes De Oca
Maps by John Fleck
Production by Que-Net Media
Printed and bound in the United States by Lake Book Manufacturing, Inc.

07 06 05 04 03
10 9 8 7 6 5 4 3 2 1

Library of Congress Cataloging-in-Publication Data
Williams, Suzanne, 1949-
    Powhatan Indians / Suzanne Morgan Williams.
        v. cm. -- (Native Americans)
Includes bibliographical references and index.
Contents: River and forest people -- Powhatan tribes and villages --
Working together -- Powhatan seasons -- Growing up -- Chief Powhatan --
New people -- Pocahontas -- Pushed from the land -- Unfair rules --
Virginia Indians -- Speaking out -- Powhatan today -- Living people.
    ISBN 1-4034-0866-1 (lib. bdg.) -- ISBN 1-4034-4174-X (pbk.)
    1. Powhatan Indians--Juvenile literature. [1. Powhatan Indians. 2.
Indians of North America--Virginia.] I. Title. II. Native Americans
(Heinemann Library (Firm))
    E99.P85W54 2003
    975.5004'973--dc21
                                    2003007475

Acknowledgments
The author and publisher are grateful to the following for permission to reproduce copyright material:
pp. 4, 5 Sonda Dawes/The Image Works; pp. 6, 8, 11 Giraudon/Art Resource, NY; pp. 7, 16 Rare Books Division/Astor, Lenox and Tilden Foundations/The New York Public Library; pp. 9, 23 North Wind Picture Archives; p. 10 Nik Wheeler/Corbis; p. 12 Courtesy of the John Carter Brown Library at Brown University; p. 13 Sharen Sun Eagle; p. 14 Denver Public Library; p. 15 Ashmolean Museum, Oxford, UK/Bridgeman Art Library; pp. 17, 22 Richard T. Nowitz/Corbis; p. 18 Bettmann/Corbis; p. 19 The New York Public Library/Art Resource, NY; p. 20 Hulton Archive/Getty Images; p. 21 The Public Record Office; pp. 24, 25 Virginia Historical Society/Richmond, Virginia; p. 26 Michaele White/AP Photo; p. 27 Courtesy of the Renape Powhatan Museum; p. 28 Kit H. Breen; p. 29 Douglas Graham/WLP Inc./NewsCom.com; p. 30 Steve Helber/AP Photo

Cover photograph by Giraudon/Art Resource, NY

Special thanks to Sandy McCready for her help in the preparation of this book.

Every effort has been made to contact copyright holders of any material reproduced in this book. Any omissions will be rectified in subsequent printings if notice is given to the publisher.

Some words are shown in bold, **like this.** You can find out what they mean by looking in the glossary.

Contents

River and Forest People

The sun is rising. A deer sips from a river. An opossum rushes home. This is Chesapeake Bay. The big bay stretches from present-day Maryland to Virginia. Here, rivers flow into the Atlantic Ocean. The ocean pushes into the rivers. Forests cover the rolling hills. Fish, **shellfish,** birds, and animals live here. So do the Powhatan people.

The Powhatan **tribes** have lived here for a very long time. In 1600, there were about 30 different tribes living around Chesapeake Bay. Each tribe has its own name, such as Mattaponi, Pamunkey, Nansemond, Rappahannock, Appomatox, and Weyanoke. These tribes did not call themselves Powhatan.

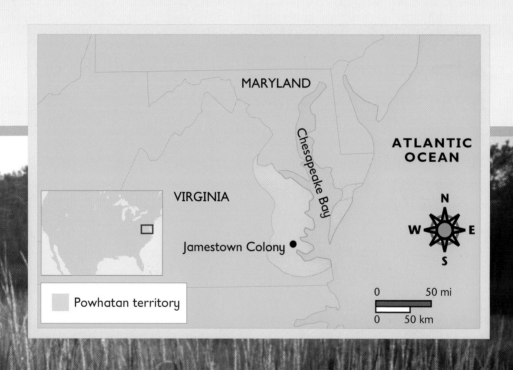

MARYLAND

ATLANTIC OCEAN

Chesapeake Bay

VIRGINIA

N

W   E

S

Jamestown Colony ●

▢ Powhatan territory

0   50 mi
0   50 km

Powhatan Tribes and Villages

Some **tribes,** such as the Mattaponis and Pumunkeys, spoke the same language. They did many things in the same way. In the early 1600s, a man named Chief Powhatan ruled many of the tribes. English people arrived in Virginia in 1607. They called all the tribes *Powhatan,* after their leader.

There were many houses and fields in Secota, a Powhatan village.

This painting shows a Powhatan man and woman eating.
It was painted in the late 1500s.

Powhatans lived in villages. Women built long, round houses. They bent wood from soft, young trees into a frame. Then they covered the frame with mats and tree bark. The village had a **temple** to honor the gods. Powhatan women planted in fields near the villages.

Working Together

Powhatans got what they needed from the land and water. Men hunted deer and small animals. They made tools, fish traps, and **canoes**. They fished in the rivers and the bay. Powhatan men **protected** the villages. Women gathered **shellfish** such as crabs and clams.

In Their Own Words

"There were so many fish that we tried to catch them with a frying pan."
—Captain John Smith, English **colonist**, 1624

Sometimes women and men worked together to plant fields in the spring.

*Powhatans often fished in canoes. They used **spears** and nets to catch fish.*

Women also gathered plants, as well as wood for fires. They made clothing from animal skins and plants. Some women **wove** warm clothing from bright feathers. Women grew corn, beans, melons, and squash. They made baskets and **pottery.** They took care of the children. The fields and houses were owned by the women who built and cared for them.

Powhatan Seasons

Powhatan life changed with the seasons. Powhatans fished and hunted all year. Women planted corn and vegetables in the spring. After the planting was done, the Powhatans left their villages. Men fished. Women gathered wild roots for food.

A New Year
Geese return to Chesapeake Bay every spring. Powhatans begin their year when the geese arrive.

Powhatans grew some of their food. They also gathered things to eat. Below are some of the foods they ate.

To hunt deer, Powhatans would hide under deerskins.
This let them get closer to the deer.

In the summer, the Powhatans returned to the villages to take care of the gardens. They picked corn and squash. In the late fall, they left again. They hunted deer and gathered nuts in the forest. Powhatans spent the winter in their villages. During the winter, Powhatans ate the food they had grown or gathered during the rest of the year.

Growing Up

Powhatan children learn from their families. In the past, girls learned what plants were good to eat. Boys learned to hunt and fish. They hunted **muskrats** and dove in the ocean for **shellfish.** Children also helped to grow crops in the fields. They might have pulled weeds or scared away birds.

Powhatan boys would have learned how to smoke fish. This kept fish from rotting so they could be eaten later.

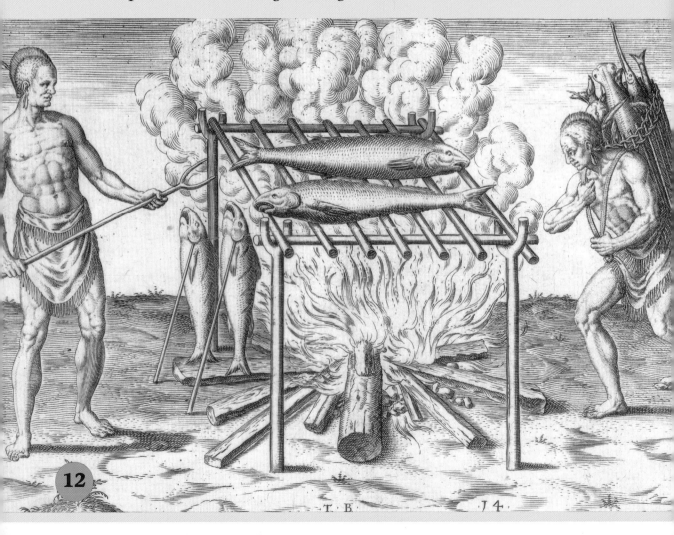

A young Mattaponi woman gets water from the Mattaponi River. The picture was made by Sharon "Gentle Wind" Sun Eagle.

Life changed for Powhatans when they were teenagers. The **tribes** had a **ceremony** for teenage boys. Older men took the boys into the forest. They might not eat for a long time. They learned to deal with pain. After the ceremony, the boys were treated as men. Girls married when they were teenagers. When a man asked to marry a woman, he brought meat, fish, and plants to her family. This showed he could care for her.

Chief Powhatan

In the early 1600s, a man named Chief Powhatan ruled many **tribes** around Chesapeake Bay. Each tribe had its own leader, called a *werowance.* Both men and women could be *werowances.* They helped Chief Powhatan make decisions for the tribes. Chief Powhatan could also tell the *werowances* what to do. **Medicine men** also helped make decisions. They asked the gods for help. Then the medicine men told Chief Powhatan what they thought was going to happen in the future.

Chief Powhatan is shown here wearing face paint.

14

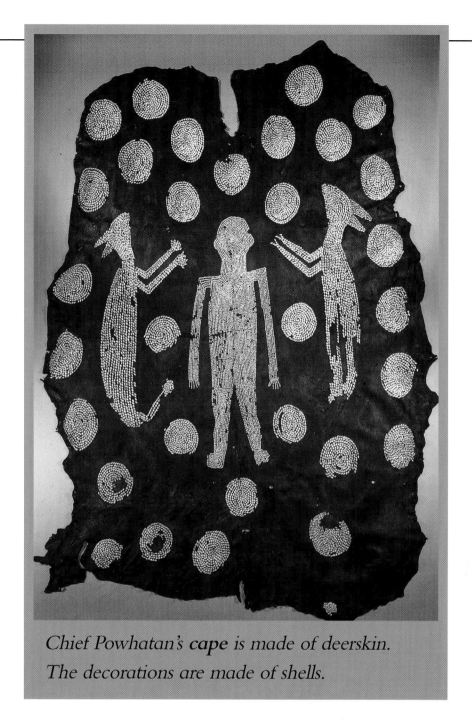

*Chief Powhatan's **cape** is made of deerskin. The decorations are made of shells.*

Chief Powhatan was powerful. It was important to make him happy. Each tribe brought gifts for Chief Powhatan. They brought him things such as deerskins, corn, and jewelry. They brought gifts to the **temples,** too. These gifts were for the gods.

New People

In the 1500s, a few strangers came to Chesapeake Bay. They were explorers from Europe. The Powhatans did not know if they could trust the new people. Soon, more Europeans came to live near the Powhatans. In 1607, English **colonists** built a town called Jamestown in present-day Virginia. These colonists wanted land so they could build farms.

This painting shows the arrival of British colonists to Powhatan lands.

*This is a **historic village**. It was built to look like Jamestown in the early days of the English colony.*

The Powhatans wanted to **protect** the land and their people. Sometimes they helped the colonists. They traded deerskins and food with them. Other times Powhatans fought the colonists. But Chief Powhatan decided the English could help him. They had guns and iron tools. The English could help Powhatans fight their enemies. The Powhatans let the English live near them.

New Animals

The English had never seen some of the animals that live in North America. They used Indian words for them, such as *raccoon* and *opossum*.

17

Pocahontas

Pocahontas was one of Chief Powhatan's daughters. She was friendly to the English. But in 1613, the English and the Powhatans were fighting. Pocahontas was seventeen when the English **kidnapped** her. They wanted to trade Pocahontas for guns and corn that they needed. The English kept Pocahontas for a year. She learned English. They also taught her about the **Christian religion.**

This painting of Pocahontas was made when she was in England. She is wearing English clothing.

Pocahontas had to become Christian before she could marry John Rolfe.

Pocahontas and an Englishman, John Rolfe, fell in love. John Rolfe wanted to marry Pocahontas. Chief Powhatan agreed. After that, the **colonists** and the Powhatans stopped fighting. Pocahontas had a son. The family went to visit England. Pocahontas got sick while she was there. She died in 1617 before she could go home.

John Smith

Many stories say Captain John Smith and Pocahontas fell in love. Others say Pocahontas saved him from being killed. These stories are not true. Pocahontas met Captain John Smith when she was eleven. He left for England when she was thirteen.

Pushed from the Land

English people took the best farmland around Chesapeake Bay. They named their **colony** Virginia. Virginia colonists paid Powhatans to use some land. They did not want Powhatans crossing their farms to hunt and gather food. Powhatans could not always find enough food on the land they had left. Some Powhatans moved away from the English. However, many others stayed.

Jamestown started out as a small village. However, soon Virginians moved west into Indian lands.

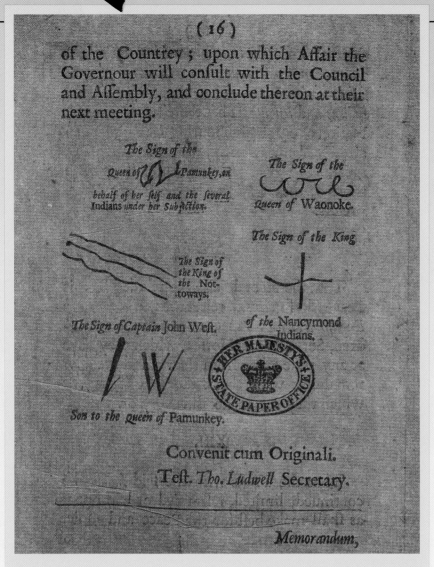

*The leaders of several Indian **tribes** signed the Treaty of 1677.*

The Powhatans and the Virginia colonists signed **treaties.** The treaties made rules about living together. Powhatans kept some land for themselves. These lands were called **reservations.** In the Treaty of 1677, the Virginians promised not to live near Indian towns. They said that the Powhatans could gather and fish on any land.

Unfair Rules

The **colonists** took almost all of the Powhatan land. By 1705, they had taken most of the **reservation** land, too. About 600 Powhatans still lived nearby. Some Powhatan men hunted and fished for the English. Some Powhatan women worked as **servants.** Others made money by selling **pottery.**

*This is part of a **historic village** in Jamestown. The woman is working on a piece of pottery.*

*Virginia colonists made some Indians work as **slaves**.*

The colonists made many rules that were unfair to Indians. After 1691, Indians could not marry white people in Virginia. Indians could not go to court if someone hurt them. Some Powhatans fought for the colonists during the **American Revolution.** But this did not change how white Virginians treated the Powhatans.

Virginia Indians

Powhatans and white people lived side by side for hundreds of years. By the 1800s, many Powhatans lived and worked like their white neighbors. All **slaves** were freed after the **Civil War.** But Virginia and other states passed laws to keep white people powerful. These laws separated white people from Indians and African Americans. This was called **segregation.** Indians and African Americans were not allowed to use the same public places as white people. They could not go to the same schools, either.

*Early Virginia **colonists** made laws that treated Indians differently from whites. In the late 1600s, Indians had to wear badges like this one when they visited English villages.*

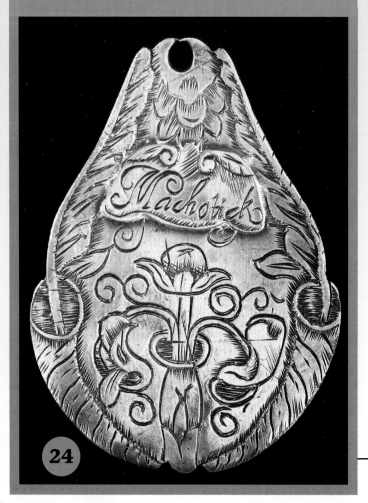

*These children attended a school on a Powhatan **reservation**. Their teacher is standing in the middle. The photograph was taken in 1920.*

By the 1900s, Virginia laws divided everything from train cars and swimming pools into places for African Americans and whites. Indians were neither. Powhatan **tribes** built their own schools and churches. Virginia Indians had to fight the laws and **officials** to be treated fairly.

In Their Own Words

"Back then a lot of Indian children did not go to school because they had to work on the farm. Many of them never got the chance to learn to read and write."

—Sandy McCready, Nansemond tribe, 2002

Speaking Out

Things changed for Powhatan people after the 1960s. A law said that **segregation** would not be allowed. In Virginia, the schools for Powhatan children closed. All children went to school together. Powhatans began to work with **tribes** across the country. They worked together to make governments keep the promises they had made in **treaties**.

Every Thanksgiving Powhatan tribes take a gift of turkeys or deer to the governor of Virginia.

Many Powhatan people in New Jersey are members of the Renape tribe. Their museum shows how Renape people lived.

A few Powhatan tribes have had treaties for a long time. The Mattaponi and Pamunkey tribes have small **reservations.** Other Powhatan people do not have treaties or reservations. But many of them still live together. In the 1980s and 1990s, some of these groups spoke out. They asked the national and state governments for **recognition** as Indian tribes.

Powhatans Today

Today people with Powhatan **ancestors** live across the United States and Canada. But when Powhatan people think of home, they think of Virginia. Several times a year, Powhatan people get together to dance and celebrate at **powwows.** It is a fun time to see friends and be with other Indians.

*Powhatan people dance, eat, celebrate, and meet friends at powwows. They are proud to share their **traditions.***

*These members of the Mattaponi tribe are working to **protect** Chesapeake Bay and the rivers nearby.*

Many Powhatans still make their living around Chesapeake Bay. They may be doctors, bankers, or factory workers. Many Powhatans fish. The Mattaponi **tribe** runs a fish **hatchery.** Powhatan tribes are also working to keep Chesapeake Bay clean and beautiful. They are fighting laws and actions that would harm the rivers they love.

Living People

Most Powhatan land was taken 400 years ago. Powhatan people lived through many hard times. Still, they have kept their **traditions.** Today, many Powhatan **tribes** are building museums and **historic villages.** Tribal leaders visit schools to tell students about their tribes. They want everyone to remember the people who first welcomed the English to North America. They want people to know that they **protect** the oldest **reservation** in the United States. They want people to know that Powhatans are still living around Chesapeake Bay.

Young Powhatans learn to keep their traditions strong.

30

Glossary

American Revolution   war American colonists fought for independence from England (1775-1783)

ancestor   relative who lived long before someone's parents and grandparents

canoe   narrow boat pushed along with paddles

cape   piece of clothing without sleeves that hangs over the back and shoulders

ceremony   event that celebrates a special occasion

Christian   person who follows a religion based on the teachings of Jesus

Civil War   war between northern and southern states from 1861 to1865

colony   land that is ruled by a distant country. A colonist is a person who lives in a colony.

hatchery   place where fish are raised

historic village   place made to look like it looked a long time ago

kidnap   steal a person

medicine man   person with spiritual power

muskrat   small animal that lives along rivers and lakes

official   person with power to carry out rules

pottery   pots, dishes, and other things made of clay

powwow   Indian gathering or celebration

protect   keep from harm or danger

recognition   when a government says a tribe has legal rights

religion   system of spiritual beliefs and practices

reservation   land kept by Indians when they signed treaties

segregation   keeping people of different races apart

servant   person who works as a maid or cook in another person's house

shellfish   animal that lives in water and has a shell, such as a clam

slave   person who was bought and sold as a worker

spear   long, straight weapon with a sharp blade at one end

temple   place to worship

tradition   custom or story that has been passed from older people to younger people for a long time

treaty   agreement between governments or groups of people

tribe   group of people who share language, customs, beliefs, and often government

weave   lace together threads or other material

More Books to Read

Ansary, Mir Tamim. *Eastern Woodlands Indians.* Chicago: Heinemann Library, 2000.

Boraas, Tracey. *The Powhatan: A Confederacy of Native American Tribes.* Minnetonka, Minn.: Bridgestone Books, 2003.

Covert, Kim. *The Powhatan People.* Minnetonka, Minn.: Bridgestone Books, 1998.

Marsh, Carol. *Chief Powhatan.* Peachtree City, Ga.: Gallopade International, 2002.

Index